The Return
of the Man Who Has
Everything

Also by Rupert M Loydell

Esophagus Writ [with Daniel Y Harris] (Knives Forks and Spoons Press 2014)
Ballads of the Alone (Shearsman Books 2013)
Encouraging Signs. Interviews, essays and conversations. (Shearsman Books 2013)
Tower of Babel (Like This Press, 2013)
Leading Edge Control Technology (Knives Forks & Spoons Press 2013)
Voiceover (Riverine) [with Paul Sutton] (Knives Forks and Spoons Press 2012)
Wildlife (Shearsman Books 2011)
A Music Box of Snakes [with Peter Gillies] (Knives Forks and Spoons Press 2010)
The Fantasy Kid (Salt Publications 2010)
Boombox (Shearsman Books 2009)
Lost in the Slipstream (Original Plus 2009)
An Experiment in Navigation (Shearsman Books 2008)
Ex Catalogue (Shadow Train 2006)
A Conference of Voices (Shearsman Books 2004)
The Museum of Light (Arc Publications 2003)

As editor:

Smartarse (Knives Forks and Spoons Press 2011)
From Hepworth's Garden Out (Shearsman Books 2010)
Troubles Swapped for Something Fresh: manifestos and unmanifestos
             (Salt Publications 2009)

Rupert M Loydell

The Return
of the Man Who Has
Everything

Shearsman Books

First published in the United Kingdom in 2015 by
Shearsman Books
50 Westons Hill Drive
Emersons Green
BRISTOL
BS16 7DF

Shearsman Books Ltd Registered Office
30–31 St. James Place, Mangotsfield, Bristol BS16 9JB
(this address not for correspondence)

www.shearsman.com

ISBN 978-1-84861-419-2

Copyright © Rupert M Loydell, 2015.
The right of Rupert M Loydell to be identified as the author
of this work has been asserted by him in accordance with the
Copyrights, Designs and Patents Act of 1988.
All rights reserved.

Acknowledgements

Advice to My Younger Self (mail art exhibition, San Bernardino, California), *Caduceus, Caught by the River, The Clearing, Creative Voice, The Delinquent, Epicentre, Epistolarium #2, E.ratio, Establishment, The Frogmore Papers, International Times, Litter, Neon Highway, New Writing, The Red Ceiling, Shearsman, Smartarse* (Knives, Forks & Spoons Press), The Spirit of Place (mail art exhibition, York, Western Australia), *The Warwick Review*.

Thanks To
Andy Brown, Peter Dent, Mike Ferguson, Daniel Harris,
Harvey Hix, Kingsley Marshall, David Miller, Alan West,
Anthony Wilson, and – of course – Tony Frazer.

Contents

1. The Other Side of Nowhere

Catching Up	13
Waiting for Luke	14
Under the Radar	15
The Burden of Proof	16
The Taller You Are the Shorter You Get	18
Fourteen Days to Pay	20
The Whole Way Through	21
Ahead of the Game	22
The Return of the Man Who Has Everything	23
On the Other Side of the Mountain	24
The End of It	26
Lipgloss & Shine	28
Karaoke Voice Removal	29
Ill-Matched	31
The Other Side of Nowhere	33
O Children	35

2. Somewhere Else

Somewhere Else	41
Noise	42
Darker than Before	43
Premonition	44
Photosynthesis	45
Complete Absurdity (Bullshit Bingo)	47
Lost Property	49
An End to Worrying	50
Dream Machine	52
Reckless	54

3. The Long Way Home

Ambulance Chaser	57
Make Believe	58
Stay Home	60
Moodometer	61
Extravagant Facts	62
Soap	63
The Long Way Home	64
Broken Circuitry	66
'My Guessed Map of a Place I Thought I Knew'	69
Staying Afloat	70
Different Maps	71
Back to Where We Came From	72

4. Ready to Fly

Saying Thank You	75
Egrets, I've Had a Few	76
Vanishing	78
No Accident	79
Outside	81
Ideas of Love	82
Boarding Pass	83
Ready to Fly	84
Advice	85
Something Has to be Done	86
Salvage	87
A Thrilling Journey	90
Just What You Need	91
Be Leaving	93
Bending the Dark	94

5. THE UNRECOGNIZABLE NOW

Just Like That	97
Standoff	98
A House Full of Clocks	99
Already Happened	100
What Are We Doing the Writing for?	102
Morning Light	104
The Unrecognizable Now	105
Another New Journey	106
Always Words	107

'I reached that odd point when you are no longer young, and yet you're still not old. You become a kind of centaur: half the person you used to be, half somebody else; that point when there is more you do not care about and less and less you do – you are in no man's land; you keep moving but not because you will get anywhere.'
– Benjamin Prado, *Not Only Fire*

'Everything that ever happened to me
is just hanging – crusted
and sparkling – in the air,
waiting to happen to you.
Everything that ever happened to me
happened to somebody else first.'
– Mary Ruefle, 'Saga'

1. The Other Side of Nowhere

'I heard some rumours about me'
– Larry Norman

Catching Up

The voices in the distance turned out to be
the radio left on so the cat wouldn't feel alone.
I coughed my way through the night
and the first hour of this morning's seminar
then called it a day. We've talked before
about how a new voice emerges on the page
among the plethora of personal and quotation,
part of the ghost society that inhabits
our subconscious when we forget to think,
which we often do. And when we do
I have to remember to think for myself
and not expect much from the others.
If you do, you're bound to be brought up
short, or find yourself diverted away
from the main route through. Are there
ways to say all this without references?
Earlier we decided so although there is
a lot of catching up implied for the reader,
who has to work on trust, hoping for
truth amongst the form, the author's
apparent involvement with text
upon the page. If you draw circular lines
in the air then you might get an idea
of the kind of thing we were discussing.
Were they letters, opinions, an interview,
an argument or an essay in disguise?
Certain questions are not worth asking,
certain answers not worth waiting for.
How can we combine these points
of view without losing emotional impact?
Or is a tree of smoke sent up by an author
enough to convince us of what we know?

Waiting for Luke

I am waiting for Luke in a pub he doesn't know
how to get to. It is probably my fault but the beer
is quite good and I have never seen it so busy.
We are both visitors, both due somewhere else
quite soon. Here he is now, larger than I remember
and panting, worried he is late and in the wrong
place. Later, Oliver may cycle over if he has time
and I might even get to the book launch I have
put my name down for. Tim and Sarah and others
I know will probably be there. Earlier, I bumped
into Bernard but now I'm not so sure which
Bernard it was, Plymouth or London? The former
would make more sense, given the warmth of greeting,
the latter because of where we are. Meanwhile,
Luke has come and gone, and a hundred students also.
Where is the man on the bike, my friend of 40 years?
How scary is that? How old am I? And why
does the depression that so many of us share
break up marriages and tear our world apart?
I would like to visit the bookstore on this woman's bag:
Housing Work, New York. And I would like to know
her name; there are far too many good looking
women out in London today. How different
this 6 o'clock pub is from our local early evening:
the whole world is present and everyone knows
everyone. Neil is jealous and wants to be here
but has urgent housing matters to deal with,
namely where to live. I can't help him relocate
from a distance, only raise a mental glass,
an actual glass, and think of friends I haven't seen
for years. The man who bursts through the door
is Oliver for a second, then clearly not. Let's hope
he turns up soon, before this poem gets too drunk.

Under the Radar

Although it seemed right at the time,
we later decided it would have been
more tactful if we hadn't. Meanwhile
the door lock became a swipe card
and the whole marking system changed.
The journey toward summer is more
convoluted and confused, no slipping
out under the radar this time it seems.

The voice of the book brings rapture
if you can keep away the sound
of the main road since they moved it
to build the new roundabout. Today,
our seminar is in a different room
and I must ascertain if the blackout
curtains work, along with the projector.
It has to be said it's a struggle sometimes,

is tempting to set fire to the forest,
burn bridges and retire before the job
gets under way. There is an undertow
of malice and contempt, a hole in my heart
where feeling should be but only the river
flows through. Mixed metaphors are like
scar tissue which never heals. I've been
here before but it wasn't that much fun.

The Burden of Proof

The burden of proof falls
on each and every one of us
as we sift through the ashes
that are all that's left
of what we used to know.
I am still unused to
the way the days bump
and knock into each other,
how every time I clear
a space it fills up right
away, every tabletop
and surface commandeered
for play, every moment
something else to do.
The sand glimmers like snow,
the unlit path leads into night;
gridded signs and arrows,
patterns of coloured lights,
do not make the approach
or touchdown any easier.
Certainty is hidden from us,
the gravel has been raked
to give the appearance of calm;
in its natural state the beach
is full of litter, a broken umbrella
collects seaweed and refuse,
bins overflow. Dogs are allowed
to roam until April the first.

Back home, black and white
papers wait to be folded,
words to be rearranged

into better shapes.
At least one book
is finished, possibly two
or three. We've been busy,
my friends and I, and
the results await publication.
Can't seem to stop the flow
but wonder where the river goes,
who reads this stuff or understands
and does it matter anyway?
She died in her sleep and that
seems the best way to go
if you have to go at all.
I'd rather show you the sky.
My daughter's young face
stares back at me from the shelf;
did we really dress the kids
like that? What will it be like
to never wake up, never write
another word? I go back to
my mother's story, but she must
feel the same: doubt around
the edge of foolish belief.
I should write a book about it
when I've ascertained the facts.

The Taller You Are
The Shorter You Get

Gravity was everywhere back then
but I didn't let it get me down.
You were so sure you could just steal
her sentence that you did. I didn't
think it was right. At weekends
I am 35, with a bright white smile,
a tight t-shirt across my chest.
It does not help you understand
if you do not turn up to class;
the idea of realism can be undermined
by cutting away all visible support
and gathering up discarded toys.
You did not understand the new book,
were waiting for UFOs to land
with medication that would work.
The paper said it was 'uproariously jolly
& splendidly inventive' but I did not
find it so, have started taking coffee
black with two sugars. Any glitches
are deliberate, designed to accentuate
the beat; any mistakes are mine.
I was listening to my past and
thinking how good it was in retrospect,
was wishing I'd kept a diary or record
of some sort. Then we hung the exhibition
and waited for our audience to come.
Which half did I paint? That would be
telling. Why do I do this kind of thing?
I couldn't say. In the soundpool
everything is looping and is plural,
the echoes wave and beckon, memory

lives in the dark. This is not the end
of the concert but it should be,
it is only feedback keeping the signal
alive and pulsing through the air.

Fourteen Days To Pay

The trouble with liking strong women
is that they come home later than you
and are tough enough to shrug off
any objections you make. The trouble
with intelligent children is that
they know when you are bluffing
and argue for their own way.
The trouble is I want to agree,
trouble is I am just in the way.
Now the air routes are open again
everyone is back where they were
supposed to have been last week
and any ash that might have descended
has been rounded up and swept aside.
The trouble with piping hot baths
is that the initial heat doesn't last,
is the way the water cools until
you just have to get out and get dry.
Goosebumps, damp towel, flaccid skin;
it's hard to get dressed or aroused,
desire seems to have been washed away,
although the midnight click of the door
signals your arrival home. High tide
produces a mirror in the valley
where we can be ourselves, living lives
that have either been flooded out
or silted up. The trouble with growing up
is growing old and knowing that we do so,
the trouble with listing your troubles
is that however many times you read them
you still don't understand exactly
how they work out the final bill.

The Whole Way Through

My book about freemasons
is hidden under the bed,
the new one about krautrock
is less defensively abandoned
on the floor. A motorick pulse
underpins most of this music,
although a recent CD anthology
reveals a surprising religiosity
at work above the beat.
There are no secrets now,
simplicity of form means
everything is available to all.
The moment of complexity
has been and gone, now
it is time to learn how to die,
having been given another
six months to live. Meanwhile,
you have handed in your notice
and are moving to the mainland,
happy to no longer be an exile
or a pirate out at sea. No,
I don't know what happened
to the poems that you sent
and no-one has bothered
to respond to my review
except for John pointing out
a name spelt wrong throughout.
This track goes on and on forever,
simply moves in circles rather than
the grid of zinc & steel squares
my new book on minimalism
so carefully describes.

Ahead of the Game

I have already marked
next year's submissions
but am worried about
timetabling the year after.
I have rehearsed tomorrow
until it has replaced today
and have forgotten to say
goodnight. You do not seem
to think it important, but
I wait for every kiss and touch,
have been visiting the future
to see how it goes. Look:
that's me, way over there.
I haven't aged at all,
have decided not to die.

The Return of the Man Who Has Everything

The man who has everything
insists upon hoarding and filing.
This morning he is collecting
drops of ink in a sketchbook
and wondering what to do
with all the young oak trees
which have sprouted from
last year's numbered acorns.
He has a boat, he has canoes,
he has too many books, CDs,
has weather fronts and systems.
How might he categorize obsession?
Why does he have so few friends
and only one lemon left for use
in the blue bowl on the table?
Using everything up is exhausting.
Why doesn't anything stand still?
And what should he do about
the man who says he has nothing
standing outside the front door?

On the Other Side of the Mountain

The war against going mad
still rages if I drink too much
or don't get enough sleep.
In the anagrams of well-being,
juggernauts drive through the night
hauling reason away. I'm still
not sure of anything, least of all
how to lay words out on the page.
What is a story? What is a poem?
Why do students assume that we know?
In the quiet war, where music
gets played to calm and fill the days,
shadows and rain can make
all the difference between
the future and what happens next.
Looking into the distance,
it is unclear if things are smaller
or bigger further away,
if the horizon is actually a line
or just a painted backdrop of
where we go to when we die.
Touring Europe is one option,
holidays on credit cards another,
avoiding patches of grease
left on the page. This is no more
than language, but I have a head
that hums in resonance with my mood,
a mind set on *loop* and *self-destruct*.
On the other side of the mountain
you will find the scaffolding
that holds up our world:

bolts and steel and wire.
If prophecy still had a voice
we might know what to do
but as it is all I can do
is plant seeds of conjecture
and hope this chronic city
never has to be built.

The End of It
i.m. David Markson

The man who constructed novels from quotes
has died and no-one knows what to use
as an epitaph or inscription on his grave.
Steve is still plundering the library for pirates,
Nathan is concerned about the use of tabs
and how they translate, or not, into html.
Tomorrow we have an awayday which will not
be very far away nor take up all of the day.
I found the office key in my shirt when I got home
and had to drive back to work, so my afternoon off
shrank to an hour before it was time to collect
the girls. In town the trousers didn't fit
and I decided I didn't need any more shirts.
They don't make cardigans like they used to,
especially if you want one in brown. This is
all I have to say and maybe my recent poems
were much more to the point: for someone
who's tired of narrative and confession
I don't half go on a bit. Out of the loop of art
and poetry it's all rather quiet though there are
several others here. Downstairs, a small person
has laid out a village street for furry animals
to live in. If you breathe too hard or slam the door
something will fall down and she will notice.
You will not hear the end of it. Each summer
there are rumours of moving the office, pay cuts
and not enough staff. Each autumn we return
to the same desks and new part-timers
who aren't sure what to do. I feel like I've
spawned a generation of writers better than me
who'll go on to greater things and find it easier

to tighten their purse-strings and belts.
If we can't agree who should lead then it had better
be us otherwise it would be them. There is never
enough sunshine to go round, and sometimes
the shadows creep in. Bob has words for empty
and words for full, it's the bit in between
which is tricky and keeps me awake at night.

Lipgloss & Shine

I like the idea of siestas
but they only send me to sleep.
It is too warm to write poems
and the gardens of the sun are dry.
If your poems are just stitched together
then how can they be in your voice?
I do not know but I can hear
inflection and tone in all the cut-ups
that we make. The colour is too
like toothpaste, squeezed over
lipgloss and shine, it is raw
and exciting, sings in the dark
but is on no account to be lived with.

Isn't it funny how stress and confusion
produce far more written work?
Traffic accelerates up the hill;
it is noisier since they built the bypass
but quicker to get into town
although I have to find a new route
whenever cars are on the school run.
Now you are moving back up north
and I do not want to bring you down
because you are so keen. It's a bloody
long way to visit and we both know
we will not make the journey very often
however hard or much we try.

Karaoke Voice Removal

'the last I heard, she had whispered in an empty room,
shut the door and then came back 10 years later
to see if she could still the whisper.'
  – anon, *Boing Boing* comments page

Quotation, misquotation, out-of-tune lyrics
sung or mumbled into the microphone,
making them hard to decipher. There is
no way to know exactly when this all started,
why meaning does not matter and why
an enthusiastic tone is all that's required.
Give me a sign, raise your hand or smile,
anything; just let me know you are still alive,
because sometimes it doesn't seem like it.
What you once whispered is still circling
in space, echoing round the stone walls of
the cathedrals and castles we abandoned
not so long ago. I am thinking of you
and hoping that you are thinking of me.
Only an expert would know about
the beginning of memory or love
although the letter from all those years ago
your mother brought down last time
makes interesting reading and reminds us
of our transitory life. Look out, somebody
told the truth and truth continues to orbit.
Cotton wool cannot keep out all the noise
or stop the phrases falling into place.
There is no exit velocity, just an increase
in noise levels, the general hubbub of the world.
Give me another sign. This time, make it
unexpected. Sing your heart out and deal later
with complaints about litter and noise.

Only an expert knows how to measure either
and they are busy someplace else.
Even if no-one listens you must not give up
on words or stop talking to yourself.
The spare champagne is in the fridge,
there is bottled water for those who doubt
and a selection of earlier writings is due
to be published soon. If I ruled the world
it would all be different, if I gave voice
to my dreams you would not know where
to look. Meanwhile, prop the door open
and let the music find its own way home.
There are fibreglass rods in the garden,
colours impossible to remember or compare,
and screams and songs out there
waiting to be listened to or heard.

Ill-Matched

Climbing walls to heaven
and gym ropes to hell;
the last few hours in my forties
and stress levels are rising
as warm-up games degenerate
into lads' football. Percussion drill
means different hands move
at differing speeds; there is the
thud of bass and cymbal's *ting*
along with echoing boys' cries.
If you were me, I wouldn't be here,
the sun would be out and
I'd be much younger still.
Even my smallest daughter says
the year's gone fast and other
parents have the same concerns.
Theo's collector's album is full
of superheroes with curious powers.
If I was them, we'd not be here
and the world's wrongs would all
be righted. The synthesizer is
off-kilter, flanged and sprung
into different shapes, tonight's
two teams are ill-matched
and prone to prejudice. In the
call and answer of this music
you have to hit the kitbag
with the ball. It doesn't bounce
and the goal is often undefended.
If it was me I'd stop running up
and down and concentrate on
passing the buck. It is usually

someone else's fault but they
simply will not take the blame.
Take a guitar solo, a drum solo,
let the singer grab a drink,
help to stretch out the evening.
If he was me there wouldn't be
an audience for this sort of thing.

The Other Side of Nowhere

'And you know the reason I really love the stars is that
we cannot hurt them.'
  – Laurie Anderson, 'Another Day in America'

Well, I guess you might have been right about that guy.
He turned out good after all, huh? Don't tell me
how the story ends, it hasn't happened yet.
Modern life tunnels under what was once solid ground,
what we assumed was *terra firma*. Don't tell me
where the path now goes, I'm far too old to travel.

It is your turn now, your world to explore,
to make and find. Start saving for next summer,
start remembering now if you want to remember anything.
This will all pass. This too. And this. Everything must go,
must go and will. Don't tell me I'm a cynic, I know
where this path leads, I am too old to be fooled.

I'm sure you will be alright, will find your own way
to right and write the world. Always remember
that language is a virus (William Burroughs said so)
and viruses mutate and then devour their host.
Nothing is stable for long: look at me, at how we live,
at how we got to here. It is an easy road to travel,

if a little complicated leaving everything behind.
I guess I was wrong about the plan, if there ever was
a plan. Talent and determination got us here,
but how will we get back home? Threshold space
is all we own, along with a sofa for guests.
You would do well to file these facts, keep them

on your shelf. Until now they have not received
scrutiny or attention, have been disregarded in favour of
a desire for intimacy and time. I know context isn't all
but I must stress the unusual nature of this guy
and how he sings his songs. The story hasn't ended
because he is a self-propelled missile on his way

to other landscapes peppering the different regions
of our world. What are days for? To keep apart
sleepless nights, to keep the sun up in the sky,
to hold the gravity which pulls down the air
that presses upon the wrong man who it seems
is me. I guess I didn't turn out so bad after all?

We've all had to make do and our story hasn't ended yet,
although it's getting close. I am so old I am often
taken for a fool or for a ride, sometimes out to lunch.
In the background in a different language plays
a different song which weaves into what we are hearing,
the sense we are making of these last few days.

O Children

'I want one of them art deco halos
just to emphasize my pain.'
  – PM Dawn, 'Art Deco Halos'

1

In the parent's dream
the youngest child
circles thought and thoroughfare;
each time he finds out something new
things get more and more suspicious,
allocated staff are redeployed
as the budget does not make sense.
It is all smiles and nods,
gestures towards meaning
and hopes that it will go right.
It won't, information techniques
will not allow this discursive mode
or any new approach.
Each dark night
I leave my silent house
and walk to school
via the quiet inlet of learning
and widening participation.
It is just another day in America
but here every moment counts
and if you do not take the test
then test results can not be published.
It is a dark time in the history
of repulsion and greed,
thank goodness the older one
made it through unscathed.
Now you will need permission

to be allowed to leave school
which will henceforth be a hut
or possibly the ruined house
of a government or queen.
O children, what have we done?
A fault line links us all,
is there anywhere more guilt or despair?
Truthfully, I wouldn't know.

2

You think you are saving the world
but you are filling up containers in India,
recycling all that has gone before.
Allocated time is full
of other things to do.
It is all similes and gestures,
no-one will take the blame,
no-one knows what to do;
they never have, they never will.
If we do not renew consumption
then how can we get greed to work?
Without greed we might be content
and learn to live our lives,
remember how to learn.
The boat needs repairs and I
do not want to canoe in the rain.
If one more stranger
wishes me happy birthday
I shall drive away
and never return,
will find myself lost again.
The postman has delivered more bills
but there is no money to be had.

It is a dark time of month:
sky overcast, account overdrawn,
no summer to be seen.
O children, what have you done?
We promised you the earth
and you took us at our word.
Take it now, go on.

2. Somewhere Else

'…the entire planet has become a whispering gallery…'
– Marshall McLuhan, 'At the Moment of Sputnik'

Somewhere Else

'He was always where he was going'
– Tim Gautreux, *Waiting for the Evening News*

Long morning shadows
stretch toward the horizon.
I let the cool air in
(shutters open wide)
to capture for later
(windows shut tight).

The hills are low and distant,
the olive trees almost white.
There is very little sound:
fridge's hum, someone turning
over in a creaking bed, the tick
of the only clock in the house.

I had to get up to find out
what the time was, whether
it was time to get up or not.
Outside, the sound of summer
exhaling, sighing, holding
its breath ready for the day.

I am always somewhere else
escaping from what I am,
always where I am going
but never quite get to.
Please wait for me there,
wherever that turns out to be.

Noise

for Gillian

All the noise in the world
can't hide your inner silence.
Harbour-side and high street
were full of people walking
aimlessly on the last night
of their hols; there were queues
at the bars and ice-cream stalls.
Your daughters didn't know what
to make of me, an old friend
from the past, and weren't sure
what to think or say about secrets
we maybe might once have shared.
Non-stop cricket seemed to help,
and our friend's strange paintings
on the wall of where we ate.
Who could resist moon-worshipping
shamans and spirit horses
with their blackbean burger?
Should we buy a camper van
and come to see you in Scotland?
Probably not. And what about
a bigger painting studio in town?
Double-dip recession suggests
the shed's still a better place to be.

Darker Than Before

The acorns fall on the roof like gunshots
and there are autumn strawberries outside.
I am ensconced in the shed, wondering
what to do now the light is hardly here
in the evenings and our jobs may disappear.
Questions have been prepared, no doubt
answers too, but they will not make
any sense, will simply be diversions,
moving the blame to somewhere,
someone else. If you want to know
the reasons you must make them up
yourself, if you want to die happy
then start practising your smile.

There are only thirty two days left
to Christmas, but I am not counting.
Say goodbye to a life full of farewells,
say hello to independent thought
and begging on the street. Fresh fruit
will help you live longer, freshen up
before you go. Some kind of shift
has happened without us really
noticing, something's gone awry.
The money has run out, so has
any inclination I had towards
regular work or an easy life.
I will paint the world white
and draw up new plans,
prepare for winter's bite.

Premonition

The fat man and his girl are in the angel's doorway,
blocking my line of sight as a moonlight voice
sings about winter. See what nostalgia does?
A hundred flowers don't want us to remember
they were there and I know you don't like failure
but these are recurrent territories we must learn
to call our own. If you look, every horse's mouth
has a silver lining. I thought this poem was going
to write itself but someone on the way to work
has dug out a pool fed by the stream and is offering
guided tours of the district: twenty miles of nowhere
in a single afternoon. He is exploiting the abstract,
directing attention to the quality of objects on display.
It is like a red rag to a bull, a bone jump shuffle call.

Only the poet is on the road to compromise
but there is no pitch control or speed display
and he is unable to discuss the texture of language
as he tries to tear it up. It is written, rewritten
and then put aside, forgotten in our perfect world.
I lost you amongst all these strangers as you hung up
the moon in a lesser heaven and wiped the rain
out of your eyes. In the cloudy breath of morning
it seemed we might finally be able to make a map
of the ocean, transform the dream and find our own
universe. No chance, not in this enchanted room
of loveless sleep and experimental soundscapes.
Thank you for making me beg. Not every clown
can be in the circus and you are my big excuse.

Photosynthesis

Peter from Devon is in Cornwall
but may not be free to meet up.
I may not be free of worry or
have time off from work, have been
tossing and turning all night, worrying
about worrying and all the things
I worry about. If you think of madness
as not being sane then I am going mad.
With desire, with worry, with whatever
it is in the air this autumn. Apparently
there's mist this morning and sunshine
later on. The paintings in the church
were 16th century, painted on salvage
from a wooden ship. I am hoping
to go for a walk but have yet to decide
on a time or a place. We are not winter
people, need more sunlight and friends.

If you define photography as drawing
with light then there isn't the problem
with his work you might otherwise think
there is. It's one way to frame a review,
one way to think about what to make
of these coloured shapes and forms.
If I read you a story will you tell me one?
If I learn to think straight can I go out
on my own? Proceed with caution.
You need to be able to discuss the text
and use examples to support an argument.
There is no wrong or right any more,
just how you decide to make your case.
This semester I will be mostly feeling sick

and will not be able to sleep. Each morning
I make myself wake up, get tea for us all,
and struggle to hold back the tears.

Complete Absurdity (Bullshit Bingo)

Sustainability Week only lasted three days,
as there wasn't enough stuff to do. Meanwhile,
we rewrote our degree in an afternoon
and pondered ideas of parity before considering
the real differences between our two sites.
We are only a bunch of excuses away
from chaos and contempt, unless you
take the bus. Nothing has been decided
but you have bought a pile of secondhand books
just in case there is nothing to read.
We needn't have worried about being lost
because they had put out photocopied signs,
but afterwards, wind and rain had been at work
and there appeared to be no maps, no logic
to campus layout or design. If we satisfy
the criteria, we may be eligible for subsidy.
Believe it or not we had to divvy up
the building costs and allocate the tarmac;
what a lesson in complete absurdity!
We have to start to say 'this is what
is happening here', begin to strengthen
our relationships and decide where we go
with the brand we seem to have inherited,
perhaps created by mistake. The media
need to be convinced, made to get it right;
only then we can sustain ourselves in the future
and start to live in peace. We can't go on
like this, there is nowhere to meet up,
only the barnlike structure that sometimes
serves up tea. We have always lived
in a half-way house, always had to make up
the time and fake the experience. We need

to be invisible, allow crossover and seepage,
embed ourselves in the infrastructure,
live in clusters which we have to create.
All facilities must be open to all and we must
change the way we use our time. Ambition
is reflected in the way we use the space,
how we use resources and barricade ourselves
into the small damp rooms we call our own.
There is the strangest kitchen I have ever seen
and I am slightly afraid of newer or bigger systems
but it may be reassuring to know that it seems more
and more likely that we will all become cross-fertilised
and able to traverse boundaries and disciplines.
We will have to make an effort and organise trips
to the other side. Beautiful hotels can facilitate
small meetings within a massive space, we can't
even get a decent cup of coffee. Can we own
a physical space, give ourselves an identity,
a presence in the world? Nowhere is completely
out of bounds and although I don't want to go on
about my own particular situation, we do need
a working model, need to allow more time
for dialogue and discussion like this to happen.

Lost Property

for Nathan

'He looks like lost property now'
  – Craig Raine, 'The Tattooed Man'

Bill was asking what my new paintings were about
and I facetiously said 'paint'. But as you observed,
just when you think you are talking about one thing
it turns out to be a conversation about something else.

One moment it's a discussion about poetry,
the next it's the mystical meaning of your name
if you translate it into numbers according to
an Aramaic scroll recently discovered by a lake.

Then it turned out to be Peter's round and
as he made the trip to the bar the talk moved on
to yesterday's television that we hadn't watched
anyway and films none of us will ever see.

I was doing my best to keep up and so were you
but it all went into a spin. Art is art and talk
is talk but if no-one knows where it is leading
then all that's left is luggage on the floor,

full of our frustration. Anyway, what a time
it's been. I've still not thanked you for the drink,
am still wondering how important it is
that the letters in your name add up to seven.

An End to Worrying

'People said it was the future then, and we
liked falling into mirrors'
   – Matthew Zapruder, 'Poem (for Grace Paley)'

The boat was as dry as dry could be
although the awning was full of holes
which hadn't let rainwater in.
I wondered how this could be
as the tide slowly covered the mud,
as the wind rose and blew me
into tomorrow, which was only
a reflection of today, still populated
by the exactly the same people.

The poem was as poetic as could be
expected but your theory is full of holes
which leave the reader adrift and lead
to bad reviews. It is hard to turn back
the tide and reinvent the wheel.
Soundbites and metaphors, similes
and asides all converge in your poems,
which you say are something to do
with truth and self-expression.

It's a bit like the ghost of tomorrow
walking into the room, a bit like
the past has happened before. The past
has happened before. I don't want to
alarm you but this rings too many bells
and I am trying to warn you, to scare
you into moving somewhere else where
there is a waterproof waterproof cover
and everyone is their own true self.

The future is as uncertain as could be
although it will probably be alright
in its own peculiar way. It is just
time passing, and the memory of things
affecting me this way, just my way
of passing the time. It is that time
of year again; soon it will all be over,
soon it will again be spring. It will take
ages to dry out, I shouldn't wonder,

forever to undo. It is the little things
that get me down, not the grand theory
of space & time, or even the price
of drinks. The same people always
seem the same to me, and the ones
we want to see live far too far away.
Everything is not connected, there is
no true sequence of lies. Tomorrow
I will try to put an end to worrying.

Dream Machine

for Tim Cumming

In our local, the folk club were singing carols
to the painful bleat of strangled pipes
and an out-of-tune guitar. We were glad
when it stopped and Dylan tunes kicked in.
Phil, you said, is doing another anthology,
then went outside for a ciggy while the vicar
and I talked about Noggin the Nog.

The world is full of undigested and unfinished
children's stories, half-remembered songs
and scraps of time. I put to you my theory
about books for kids and prose poems
sharing a pared-back clarity; today
you told the students how poetry
informed all your reviews and articles,

how everything you write is true,
but only some of it is fact, had ever
happened to you. It puzzles them,
this world of words they are tiptoeing into,
they still want to *self-express*, *be honest*;
have far too much to say and are afraid
to let language do its work for them.

Behind the lectern you looked like Steve,
a good-looking shadow of gesticulation.
The film flickered behind you, above you,
around you, your voice part of the texture
of colour and sound assembled elsewhere.
In the cave of knowledge it is dark,
but you have been there and drawn it.

I'm drawn to it but my lunchtime meeting
provided a different point of view, someone
at a distance, who did not want to speculate
or even read the facts. If we make a network
complex enough then we will give birth
to thought; it is a matter of size, surety
and science. Parataxis and parentheses

should not be encouraged, argument
and attitude must be kept at bay. He would
not shake my hand or look me in the eye.
What would he make of the dream machine
you captured in your film? Or the roses growing
from your mouth as you read William Burroughs
aloud in the cold, half-empty lecture hall?

Reckless

The first time we saw him on TV
we couldn't believe how ugly he was.
All pout and powder, feathers, flares,
bombastic falsetto full in your face.
He wanted to to go somewhere
and he did. By next time
he had become someone else,
prettified and personable,
a pantomime dame of pop.
Today is the highest tide
and lowest temperature
of the year. I am hoping it
won't freeze again; last night
I was up a ladder pouring
hot water over a frozen pipe
until the heating came back on.
Dean Young is the only one
who can almost convince me
surrealism should be taken seriously,
is worth a second-look. Pushing
process and reason aside,
he is reckless in his argument
and use of quotation, seems
to want it every way, like me,
although I bet he hasn't got
a septic finger from the cactus
in my studio. I have, and it hurts;
bleeds if you squeeze it hard.
Here comes another cold snap,
here comes another wave
of would-be bands with attitude,
another day of tutorials,
demonstrations and disturbance,
another scab and fineline scar.

3. The Long Way Home

'Those lives
were probably someone

else's, but it pleased us
to pose alongside them.'
   – Mark Bibbins, 'Viva Isabella Blow'

Ambulance Chaser

This morning the rain corporation is muttering
many things. Grey things, damp things,
things that flow from one idea to another,
from year zero to the future via now.
It all began back before we knew
what it was would happen but then,
before we knew it, it happened anyway;
we all became nostalgic and misty-eyed,
which didn't help our driving or reading
but there was a bit of a sparkle in low light
and it gave me a subject just when needed,
as I am now the only one not doing research.

It is no longer new and there is nothing
left to say or do. I will never be ready
and neither will you. There is all the time
in the world and it is running out,
there are stress fractures appearing
in my life, recklessness cannot begin
to describe how we will have to live.
I'm not chasing after an ambulance
but there's an accident waiting to happen.
We are watching our own car crash
onscreen, sitting tight in the snow
waiting for a slow-motion rescue.

Make Believe

'Take my voice. I don't need it. Take my face
I have others.'
 – Ben Lerner, 'Mean Free Path'

Twenty-plus years of make-believe hidden
in a box. Occasionally a book comes out,
sometimes words escape. It is a long way
to come for nothing, a waste of time
and money if you have other things to do.
Regular pay does not make up for the loss
of effort and ambition, any more changes
will kill me; I need certainty and surety,
family and friends. Do you remember
the people we used to know? Do you know
the people I used to remember? In the room
down the hall, a winter journey away,
there is a secret but I am not telling you
what it is, only that it is there. It is impossible
to work out why we are no longer in touch.

You suggest it is distance, lack of time
or having children, disinterest or disdain;
or perhaps it is another story to do with
something I once said or matters of class
and wealth? We are under great pressure
to achieve, all offered ladders to climb,
but they are steps to nowhere, to dreams
that no longer exist. In tomorrow's music
everything makes sense, the events of sound
constitute the event. Managers create change
as an end in itself before quickly moving on.
We will be left to clear up, are the ones
rumbling the piano or bowing the cymbal,

scraping tunes out of anything we can find
that hasn't already been sold as scrap.

Stay Home

The longer I live here the less I want to.
This morning's snow was followed by
rain and thunder, then more snow;
it was difficult to know whether
to go to work or stay home with the girls.
In the end the bus didn't come anyway
and there was an email from on high
telling us all to stay away. We did,
but then letters started arriving
offering redundancy and cuts in pay.
It seems they have lied to us
and do not have our best interest
at heart, seems promises were made
they had no way of keeping. So hallo
to misery, servility and falsehood,
where we live on an unsure footing
halfway between poverty and despair.
It is a long story and I will bore you
another time. Change comes in
a plain brown wrapper as dreams arrive
then go. We have not got it made,
even though we were getting it right,
it is simply that others disagree and have
a different map of things in their head.
The longer they are here, the more
I know how much I don't want to be.

Moodometer

What a difference a day makes…
One moment it's working, then not.
The plumber says he is giving up
plumbing, can't cope any more.
What's on the moodometer today?
How is the graph? Please don't
tell anyone unless we say you can.
You can't. We are two toilets down
and not in the mood; besides,
I have a stinking cold and lots
of marking to do. All it is is brass
to plastic connections. If they would
stop leaking it would be OK. There is
nothing specific getting me down,
I'm just down. You must use quotes
more specifically, this reads like
a freeform rant not an academic essay.
Why don't things work like they used to?
We never had these problems before
and if we did we've carefully forgotten.
The other plumber will be here next week,
until then use the downstairs toilet.
Yes, I know it's cold. Make the line
slope up and email a friend to say why
the carpet is up to dry and no-one
is using the leaking shower. Is there
an alternative to plotting lines?
Only drugs we don't want to take
or holidays we can't afford. Continue
to plot the failed connections between
the days, the way the world falls
apart the moment you start
to breathe in the morning air.

Extravagant Facts

Pinned paper pictures
to the wall, then took
them down, unconvinced
they were anything more
than sketchbook scribbles.

I am going to follow the sun,
walk around the room and
sieve sand onto the floor,
make an oasis and wait for
a glimpse of evening light.

So why do I still make
these constructs of colour,
why groom these transmissions
into something approaching
a memory of order?

Extravagant facts explain nothing.
Better to smudge and stain
as gravity falls and night
brings the end to another day,
hides our impossible forms.

We are already there, away
on a field trip finding out
that there are no answers,
just whispers from the angels
and shadows here below.

Soap

I like the way this soap I've just opened
has SOAP stamped on it. Bad science fiction
has info dumps to explain to the reader
how worlds work; onscreen that means
signs everywhere. Why doesn't the sky
have SKY written on it in the clouds?
Why doesn't the wall have THIS WAY UP
in contrasting bricks? If I was dyslexic
words might appear broken up, interrupted
by globes of light. Since I'm not it doesn't
and I know the names of most things I use.
It's good to know that soap is soap and
words is words, at least most of the time.

The Long Way Home

three lessons for Norman Jope

Lessun 1: to write speach yoosing speach marks

The sad part of me has been downloading progrock
without anyone knowing; all twiddles and beeps,
long solos and sighs from high-pitched voices
at the back. You mention Eno, Ligeti and others,
and I can see a link: your past spent elsewhere
but the same memories catching up with us both.
Here, we don't let go of memories, let alone
toys we no longer play with. There is no room
for books and clothes or all our other things.
If we do not put stuff away before anything else
comes out, there will be no floor to stand on;
if we walk only in the shadows, on the cracks
between slabs, we may be able to find
a dry path into the future. The plumber
has still not been but I have been rereading
your prose poems and listening out for bells
as darkness falls and today's six-part epic
finally comes to a guitar-splintering end.

Lessun 2: to make tishew paper coco beans

Over here is my collection of triangular stones
and here green, blue and clear smoothed glass
picked up by the sea. Here, round pebbles
and there, tangles of coloured fishing net.
Hidden in the loft, a pair of small red wellies
and the air that was trapped between us when
we first held hands. Now her tooth has fallen out

she can whistle through the gap at the front,
give voice to all her fears about going to school.
Music is not on her agenda; play and chocolate are.
Maybe the plumber will come later and remind us
again how lucky we are to have hot water at all;
his house very rarely gets up above ten degrees.
We should be tougher, stop whining and get on
with our lives. The kind of thing people say
when they want to not get on with their job.

Lessun 3: to take away elevun from thees numbers

The hidden part of me stays inside and lets me cry
outside. Apparently there is no grand conspiracy
and management wish to have more dialogue,
in a spirit of partnership. This does not mean
anything has changed. How dare you question
the plan. We have invented it and will follow it
through, though it makes no sense at all.
Turn off the mains, let everything dry out;
put these boxes in the loft. It is better to hoard
than to let things be given away. Out at sea,
steel islands wait to become private kingdoms;
in each suburb a principality dreams of its past.
Utopia is just an idea, but there is no reason
not to make a triple album of songs about it.
We could navigate any city in the world
with just a drum kit and a doubleneck guitar,
can always find the longest way back home.

Broken Circuitry

Now that rust isn't a problem we park our cars
on the drive and fill up the garage with junk.
If you make only the minimum payment
it will take you longer and cost you more;
if you make only the minimum effort
it is likely your grades will suffer.
Today it is warm enough to canoe;
the heron and egrets are out fishing
on the creek, and I am waiting for
the evening news to beam in from afar.

Now that we know how to fix the car
I keep a spanner under the seat,
a bottle of water in the back,
am well situated to sabotage understanding
and devoted to experiencing the moment,
extending my monumental vision and
encouraging outrageous audience involvement.
I have an ingenious knack for manipulating
layers of feedback into melodic hums and buzzes,
am angry at being written out of my own history.

Now, *that's* spontaneous architecture:
buildings put up without planning consent,
sheds and outbuildings everywhere,
all out of keeping with the view.
We have been punished for remaining
ourselves, attracting public attention,
encouraging radical disorder,
for which I believe there is a lack and a need.
If you perpetually deal in hints and clues
then you lose all clarity of definition.

Now that it's deemed okay to write poems
I quickly got another book together and
did a second review of that anthology
because I want to be in the next one.
Let's hijack the bookselling business
and infiltrate the best-seller charts.
It is enough to make you scream
and start a new conspiracy theory,
if only they would let us. I've had to
smuggle this out, every paranoid word.

Now that they are back in power
we can have a perfect train wreck,
can derail the economy and start
to really screw things up. Get in line early
and rattle your cage; this is a crazy world
full of living room wars for no reason why,
different guitars for different tunes,
tapped telephone calls, fire in the sky.
The tide is rising, let's make the water black:
that's how every empire falls.

And now that that's completely clear
let's work to to make it happen:
sign in at visitor reception then proceed
to the sports hall where you must choose
an option. Only, there are no choices left
because they think that they know best.
We'll never know how their minds work
or if they work at all. It is up to us
to find knowledge pointing towards
possibility interwoven with sound.

No matter what the artist's intention,
I'm still looking and listening,
laughing and crying. But underneath
I'm scared. Whatever is twisting
in my mind and testicles is nothing
but reflex action, stress and despair
outside the range of understanding.
I am left clinging to uncertainty,
all optimism glitched and phased
into an oblivion of broken circuitry.

'My Guessed Map of a Place I Thought I Knew'

for Zac, who drew it

Over here is nothing
and back where I started
is somewhere else.
I used to be at home here
but now I barely remember
the house I lived in,
school, or even where
I learnt to play guitar.

Drive towards Land's End.
The land ends there
and you must drive back
the way you came,
but down the bigger road
that bypasses all the coves
I'm sure I've visited
but don't know the names of.

I took my new motorbike
back to see where I had been,
to find out if my past
was still there. It wasn't,
it isn't, and everywhere
is simply nowhere now,
a map full of empty spaces
and a whole lot of don't knows

Staying Afloat

The boat seems to be taking forever
and the coffee has burnt on the stove.
I have learnt to paint in five minute bursts,
become used to bitterness and fingernails
that can never be got clean. The smell
of barbecue lingers although it is not really
warm enough for shorts or al fresco living.
I have drunk red wine and watched the sunset,
drunk lager and played table football, drunk
sparkling wine and now I have run out
of easter holiday. Varnish over the screws,
the truth and don't worry about the small split
in the side of the hull: once it is in the water
it will swell up and everything will be alright.
There are stripes of pink and blue sky
in the sea towards St Ives, there are spots
in front of my eyes and the sun has not yet
burnt through the morning haze. We will
break our journey here, rest a while and then
move on. At last we are ready to sail.

Different Maps

Noise maps squeal into existence
as a car drives out in front of me.
I brake hard and think of you,
looking forward to having you home,
to reinventing the landscape we share.
I throw away an unopened loaf,
call by work to fill in some forms,
then try to settle down and read.
But the drums next door distract,
pluck at my concentration;
any focus I had is gone.

If we draw a line between us
and all the people we know
we end up with black marks on the page
and white noise in our heads.
It has been a long four days;
I am not used to silence any more
and have had to learn
how to walk through shadows
usually full of conversation,
loud music and argument.
Any focus I had is gone.

Back to Where We Came From

Built a boat that has never sailed;
can't move my leg enough to launch
or crew. I am in London but I'm not,
I'm here, with words on the screen.

What did we make of art & text this morning?
Haven't got a clue. Hardly anyone was there
except those who were. But it's good to read
the first two reviews although they're only blogs.

Another tide has started to ebb. It's not been
dry or windy, warm enough, to make the effort
to go for a sail. Alan didn't answer his phone
and by the time he did I was in the pub,

lunching alone, except for Bill, who made it
two. I didn't get to read the books I took
or today's newspaper. Jeff Koons' sculpture
is like a scrawl of coloured paint in air,

I like it very much. And even though
you do not know who Agnes Martin is,
tomorrow I am driving to see her work,
having not been in London or Exeter tonight

where one of my favourite singers is singing
and all my friends will be. Adrift in time,
with a new wall of paintings nobody wants,
I note how much I enjoyed the steak.

4. Ready to Fly

'This, too, is a window. If I jump
I'll fall into my own arms.'
— Yannis Ritsos, 'Morning'
(tr. David Harsent)

Saying Thank You

for & from Sandra

How very curious this furtive plopping,
this birthing of what might be detritus
or on the other hand might be a project.
On the other other hand (I have too many hands)
a set of notes or a variousness of opinion,
a little play in colour. As I was sitting at my machine
draped in a violent green cardigan, I was roused
but not aroused by the thwumping of pavement
meeting postman's feet, the kerrang of the metal gate,
the cruel rippling shove of paper against metal.
Eventually, roused enough to rise, I am to be found
tearing at an envelope with your writing on it,
while feeling the small rectangles captive within.

What a curious thing is this receiving unasked.
Exciting, alarming, yet at the same time carrying
the seeds of disappointment. I feel I have not passed
the test, although there is no test. I enjoy the format,
the folding, the colour, the shall I say style.
I am removing myself to the summerhouse, to unfold
and inspect. I feel admiration for the spirit notes,
but they do not ask me for anything. I do not go easily
into the whale world, but find I move through it rustily,
jaggily, much as the paper through the slot.
I am lost in eeees. I could count them, but won't.
Mmmm, aaah. I do not know. I am not saying
I may or could never know, just that I do not.
I can keep folding and unfolding my brain train drain.
This is where I say thank you: Thank you.

Egrets, I've Had a Few

for Nico Muhly

Bill said he'd read my new book
and had decided egrets was code
for something else, that I meant
to write about much more
than birds. In the mothertongue
language is garbled and skewed,
words run together in the archive
and make a monster out of sound.

After the wonders of new things
made from old, comes the only tune,
a style drift of interstices
and seizure, a cracked folk song
sung early Monday morning,
well after the pubs have closed,
a conversation in sign language
onlookers do not understand.

Last night the sky was wild
with the only music it knows:
rain and lightning, grey cloud
and thunder to wake the dead,
the kids at least. I must admit
I have misunderstood my work,
perhaps because language itself
is showing signs of stress:

all those gospel outbreaks,
apathetic ponds of doom
and abstract nocturnes
produce a dark turn of mind.

It's the same old same old…
the knight takes the bishop,
the rook takes the queen
and it always end like this.

Vanishing

These shoes were inspected by D
but sunshine is disappointingly elusive;
after several days of rain
it is difficult to know what to wear.
Memory slopes toward the future
but it is hard not to slide back
into what might have been
or could have been
if things had been different then.

You didn't even say goodbye
but neither did I. All we want
is to get back to basics
and to know when summer will be.
All the talkers are talking tonight
about how the moon turned red
but my shadow follows me
even in the dark. Tiny losses
register at the edge of my vision:

yesterday has gone and today
we are home because the electricity
is off at work. There is a scarcity
of miracles but music tries
to convince me otherwise.
The price we pay for secrets
becomes the debt that we incur;
I feel as though I am vanishing
as the world swallows me whole.

No Accident

'And you may ask yourself – Well…
how did I get here?'
  – Talking Heads, 'The Great Curve'

It is not the one I wanted and this is not
where I want to be. It is too large or small,
the wrong colour, will not fit into my bag.

Delete as seems appropriate and look at
the curve of the towel's shadow on the wall.
Pay no attention to the man behind the curtain.

We are guided by voices who are guided by
those unable to see how the tower will fall
if we don't put our cards down right.

The leaflet seems to indicate that nothing
has changed, that everything is the same,
when of course it is totally different.

There are no accidents any more, just things
that happen by themselves caused by
butterfly wings the other side of the world.

We walked to the end of the island to wonder
at high tide, both sides, both channels full.
Geese and ducks, floating gulls, ignored us,

the sun continued setting as an overloaded canoe
made its awkward way back to the quay.
It was a summer of not doing very much,

of hoping for things to happen which didn't,
a time of waiting for good weather to arrive
and for rain and air pressure to conspire.

We read instead, but the wrong books:
they didn't tell the stories I needed to hear,
were not the ones I wanted to love

and keep upon my shelves. Like them,
this is ghostwritten, best viewed with subtitles
and the sound turned down completely.

I am probably someone else entirely,
can only catch glimpses of myself in the mirror
waiting for something to make this life worthwhile.

Outside

The courtesy car ran out of fuel
and she said I was bolshy on the phone.
I wasn't meant to hear that but
she left the mouthpiece uncovered
while she told her boss. The rain
is back after three days of sun,
it is hardly daylight this morning.
The postcard from the girls
says *Keep calm and carry on*
and it is a carry on, no longer
makes much sense to me,
the way that we live now,
this weather, the children's toys
being put into the loft,
the wind in the trees outside.

Ideas of Love

I am living my life online
while a neighbour
quietly climbs the walls
and my mother misses
seeing me very much.
You arrive in the pub
with sketches and poems,
a sprawl of images and ideas
you're trying to reign in
while your partner
slowly goes mad. The drink
doesn't help either of us
and declaring visionary verse
over the folk club's blues
brings only raised eyebrows
and friendly derision.
How hard it is to be loyal
to friends who don't fit in
in the village, to ideas
of love in this world.

Boarding Pass

And here's the ego talking:
Did you ever use my poems
in class like you said you might?

My travel plan does not preclude
diversions or different trajectories;
this is not a boarding pass.

By focussing in on the decay
we draw attention to the structure
revealed through crumbling walls,

the infrastructure if you like,
the way it was originally built.
How the past has followed us:

one of the voices used in this volume
is there only to quietly catalogue
the discarded items of the dead.

If you read the newspapers
then you will know that poems
should look like this. It is easy

to take it one stage further
and promote a more fluid approach
to life. What advice do you have?

How should text perform in the world?
And did you ever use my poems
in class like you said you might?

Ready to Fly

The spirits hovering over the ashes
are vultures circling the debate.
We are just selfish, each echoing
each other in each other's minds.

The problem is not deception
but corruption. The art of mirrors
is a lie, the truth is in an envelope,
unnoticed just inside the door.

We are principled but not transcendent,
live without hope of a sensible answer.
Some are jubilant, others more sombre,
most a series of imperfect erasures

revealing an astonishing white wall.
Content arises as much from process
as from subject. That process disrupts
the poem, readers are likely to flounder.

The spirits hovering over the ashes
are vultures circling our remains.
No one wants to talk about
the echoes in each other's minds.

Advice

'How fast the blood marks us'
  – Renee Ashley

What advice would I give myself
if I spoke to the younger me?
Love more? Love less?
Keep going boy? Most of it's
gone well but maybe I
should have done exactly
what I wanted, or perhaps
have given in sooner and
got a proper job? Would
the kids have preferred
a younger Dad? Could I
have had a different life?

How come only humans imagine
alternate realities and worry
about death or how to live?
Knowing is a kind of curse;
our most special moments
always tainted and spoiled.
Looking in to the distance
I only see me, back then
and now. It's too late
to change the world
but you still have time.
Listen, take my advice:

Whatever you do, don't do it;
don't ever become me.

Something Has to Be Done

You think it is mid winter but then the sun comes out;
you think it is spring then wake up to mist and rain.
It will be warmer here than Greece or Spain,
will be quieter here now that you have gone.

While you are away the television is on
and the children have not gone to bed.
Beggars on screen are sifting through rubbish
while idiots raise money to stop them.

It is not funny and the price of beer has risen
along with car and income tax. I do not understand
how to budget and I do not know what to do
about the starving people. If I ignore them

they will go away and we will have to endure
all of this nonsense again next year. We cannot
reduce death and birth rates in the next few months
and I do not know how we can afford a holiday

this summer: because I already have too many
they turned down my credit card application.
I do not like making lists or bringing myself
into poems but something has to be done.

Salvage

I am unriddling the world.
My secret history is on the shelf,
neither secret nor much of
a history, just a line of books
I brought into being, some words
and pictures in print. Do not
assume it is true, that this
ever happened, let alone
that I meant what I said.

Grey skies followed me here;
cold memory. I am with name,
am not myself today. We used
to sing on long car journeys
but now it is headphones
and music in the back seat,
child songs and debris,
wind sweeping the way ahead,
clearing out the future.

Everything gets me down
these days as teenage gravity
pulls me toward the dark star
that turns my brain to static.
It is perfectly simple: the river
is dry, the tide is out, time
itself is malfunctioning,
nothing is the same,
whatever everyone says.

New ceremonies have replaced
the old and there will be no rest
until the chambers and valves
of outdated systems
have been removed
and the black light shines
with answers and holy noise
from above. The winter storms
that followed me here

mean happy pills and dreams;
you were supposed to sing
aloud and not be a stranger.
Out on the road, paper planes
fly through traffic fumes
as the future folds itself
into new shapes and echoes
of itself. In the gap between
thoughts, the smiles of those

who have been away but cannot
remember. Two or three fireflies
light the way and I want to go
where I belong or where perhaps
I used to. The slow lattice of prints
on the damp path is only me
going to the compost heap
and back, the music you can hear
is only diagonally talking echo.

Sometimes I make myself invisible
and watch the shadows grow,
crawl after you into memories
of boats and beaches, dusk
across the fields, and the skies

in 1982. These are dying thoughts
you don't deserve, ruins of a life
I hoped to hear the morning say;
but all I got was freezing rain,

low drones in the distance and
recycled images like this.
We all know that you have been
and gone, all know this weather
is normal for November and that
someone stole the stars and moon.
I have been tongue wrestling
with myself and lost, am
more fragile than I thought.

There once was a time
when everything made sense
and there was a reason to be;
there once was a time
when it was just a scratch
and we would never bruise.
I would like to run right back
into the stories I heard you tell
and risk the things I don't recall,

am prepared to do anything
that would bring you back.
All these years gone and I
still don't know the words for love
or how to grieve and let you go.
It is never ending, this cycle
of love and loss, drink and despair.
I am back at your door, belong
to you. Don't argue, rescue me.

A Thrilling Journey

We must choose between
a well signposted theological motorway
or an equally valid road to divinity,

must synchronise inner time
and not disagree on too many answers.
No one can predict which ones.

What is the rational response?
Just throw the book aside
and improvise the rest.

Say nothing for a while;
every journey needs to be fuelled
by some sort of passion or obsession.

I am an art critic in the mornings
and an electro heartthrob in the evenings,
preoccupied with unfinished projects.

Life, however, is a trick of light,
a task for frail and ghostly survivors
languishing in shadow.

On the one hand there's no Arcadia,
on the other our hearts are set
upon making something great.

Hardly an advertisement for holiness.

Just What You Need

You go to a seminar
you aren't really interested in
and the experience almost paralyses you
so that you acquire a nervous habit
which results in a scuttling motion
and letting the door slam on your way out.

Later, having attended a range of workshops
you badger your father to fund a convoy
to somewhere else, with the potential
to create a better learning environment.
You decide to look at certain things
upside down and back to front.

The gist of worthwhile thoughts
runs docile through your mind;
you get a glimpse of heroic men
writing of their experience as children
and are inspired by events and things
you witnessed on this morning's news.

Behold the power of language:
these poems are subtle renditions
hoisted straight from the heart
into the workshop and classroom.
In the foothills of my mind
ambivalence is king.

In the tussle between making and finding,
contradictory testimony and eloquent vocabulary,
there is a direct line from mentoring to mayhem.
You may have come to the wrong place,

might be a superior order of being;
have been brainwashed for years.

Every funeral turns into a protest,
every excursion into a procession.
There is no advantage to being committed
but it is a most beautiful experience.
Elaborate tools are unnecessary,
art assimilates emotion.

The future is words; look, we just made it.
It requires no purchase or submission
just instinct and sensitivity. I am overwhelmed
by all the projects I'm currently working on,
but it is an antidote to the rush of
unwanted data I find myself sifting through.

If we develop a model of anti-social networks
then we might eventually find a place
where we can get on with ourselves.
Our real work here is not yet done,
the question remains unasked.
This could be just what you need.

Be Leaving

No trace. The earth beneath
is an eye opener; my inhibition
well known and much quoted.

Puncture the silence. Five minutes
too early and change is on its way;
three steps at a time and you will

be homesick for liturgy and ritual.
There go the ships, laden with
something awfully like serenity.

I glance quickly at my watch.
This concerns foresight and after,
looking at where we are.

Let me be him. There is nothing
knocking on the sky now
except faded faith and rain.

Bending the Dark

If you lie awake stargazing,
the new day comes along,
fog bound and windwards,
following the offshore breeze.
It is a kind of reunion
at the world's end, a new future
from far away over the hills,
where love is real and nothing's
changed except the tideline
and the mooring fee.
I was up at five and on the quay
before six, checking the boat
and pretending the moon
was the morning sun.
Don't mind me
when you walk on my grave,
I've already forgotten
tomorrow's promises
but know we should be swimming
towards people you remember
as voices in the grooves
between one track and the next.
I have a pocketful of fire
and postcards already written
ready to send you this summer.
What will happen already has;
what hasn't never will.

5. The Unrecognizable Now

'Where we all end up, love only knows'
– Peter Dent, 'Magic Orders'

Just Like That

To tomorrow from today
is as far as I can see
or imagine. Mountains
have to be climbed
but as pink turns to blue
I remain afraid of the future
and worried about the past.

If we are to avoid disaster
then I must return home
and live happily ever after,
must find a way to be content
and learn to learn, want
to be here as night and day
roll on in voluntary abandon.

I cannot keep this up,
too many tapes are lost,
connections not maintained.
It was only a box of postcards
but it was how I organised my life;
pictures count for something,
perhaps for everything.

Bits of broken glass and rusty metal,
a circle of bronze and clay,
were all I had from back then,
and now they are gone.
No more memories. Tomorrow
is already there, if we can make it
through another empty night.

Standoff

The grass snake was back this summer,
in a standoff with the cat, and Diane Keaton
showed us all just how gorgeous and sexy
older women can be, but you still refused
to act your age although Yan was excited
about driving to Exeter to see Kelly Joe Phelps
and the papers were full of olympic events.

Kingsley didn't answer his phone
and his email box seemed to be full.
How do you contact your friends when
this kind of thing keeps happening?
How can we publish new research
if we can't even read the map of our lives?

All the money we had was plastic,
abandoned on the play room floor,
and the sunshine lasted a week at most.
We got up too late to beat the crowds,
too early to have had enough sleep,
and found ways to do nothing at all;
watched the cat dragging a stick towards us,
which turned out be a dead snake.

A House Full of Clocks

A house full of clocks, but no time
for living. Hours spent at work
don't add up, it's difficult to find
space to write and paint. Mark talked
about only doing specific projects,
already knowing there's a place to show
or send his work. Now there's a plan.

In the elephant pool behind the cathedral
the water is storm-flushed and dark.
The lights in the pub go down,
making it too dark to write or read;
now we must focus on drink.

Low clouds have infiltrated the city,
filled the street and muffled the night.
If I'd wanted to drink in the dark
I'd have stayed at home and turned
the lights off. If I'd wanted to drink
outside I'd have lain in the garden
and let alcohol and mist embrace me.

Already Happened

'Those who have written poems and stories have hidden riddles and whispers in the folds of the future.'
  – David H.W. Grubb, 'Where Will We Put the Words?'

The future has unfolded
and it has already happened.
The answering back, I mean;
this compulsion to create
on the back of what
you have written and said.

However hard I try to ignore
your words, deciding I will not
let them into my life, they
make their way off the page,
past the torn paper edges,
into my breath and skin.

Brain can argue all it wants
but it has already happened,
the answering back I mean,
the wondering about wonder,
the asking of endless questions
about the questions being asked.

I read again of orchards and
war zones, of invisible music
and the mutterings of a voice
that is not my own nor yours.
Where will we put the words?
Here, there, everywhere,

wherever they might be found,
sometimes where they won't be,
ever. But mostly they will be
set out neatly on the page,
where we might expect them,
but saying something else.

What Are We Doing the Writing for?
for David Grubb

Well, goodness knows. You've given me
thirteen possible answers, but they don't help.

I feel like the single red line on a sheet of grey,
a car driving the wrong way on the motorway,

am waiting for a tender stranger to stop
and ask if I'm okay. I'm not sure that I am,

in between work and home I just resonate and be,
try to put language in the right order

hoping there are readers out on Revelation Drive.
Why do you keep on asking if you already know?

Explanation and worry are glitches in the soundtrack
to my life, the phased guitar that slides in and out

of hearing. I sneak out of the back door
but there is nowhere to go away from words

and more will be arriving very soon. Welcome
to the world, say hello to the uninvited,

to more questions and piles of unread books.
Maybe the writing is doing us or maybe

the real question is where we will put the words
but I see you have already asked that too.

No more night letters, save your messages for day.
All matter flows but gravity will always win,

things fall out of use and drip down out of sight.
How fragile and how fierce your questions often seem.

Morning Light

I went down to the creek this morning,
instead of going straight to work,
to try and find a reason to live here.
Cold clouds covered the sky and waders
strutted their stuff. The boat was bone dry
despite the wet, and I had the place
to myself. That's often how it is
out of season, when the village seems
half-abandoned and we hide ourselves
in badly built bungalows and hope
the sun will come out soon, or at least
it will stop raining. I've only just got used
to it being this year and soon it will
be over. You don't want to be as old
as you are and haven't the girls
grown up fast? Work and pay conditions
never get any better, and since I won't
have any pension I'm not sure why
I'm doing it anyway. Tonight, it is raining
again and the wind is blowing a gale.
Dustbins clatter outside and an owl's
busy calls remain unanswered.
The future will most likely turn out
to be simply more of the same,
with nowhere to go in the mornings.

The Unrecognizable Now

In the unrecognizable now
we take on trust
that things will not change
for the worst, that we will
not wake up to find ourselves
silenced or maimed.

In the unrecognizable now
it is hard to know
what to say to strangers,
sometimes even ourselves.
It is as though the words
have slipped out of reach

into the unrecognizable now
where the simplest drone
holds far more possibility
than the bang and clamour
of yesterday's songs
or the music in my head.

In the unrecognisable now
today is where we are
and we must deal with it
or become what was before.
Outside in the frozen garden
our cat stalks hungry birds.

Another New Journey

Another new journey
proposes itself
as the words close up
and the poem loses stanzas
to become a thin line
down the page.

Where the light stops
shadows start
and we have learned
to tell invisible stories
about what might
or might not live there.

In summer's quiet evenings
shade is woven blue
and fuzzy, but winter's
corners are black and dark,
cannot be presumed empty.
Come spring, this is

all forgotten, forgiven,
as new life begins,
another long journey
to the end of the year,
like all the other ones
we've made before.

Always Words
for & from China Marks and Harvey Hix

Was it always words for you?
It was always words for me.
I was a great, omnivorous reader
as a child and adolescent,
and I've written all my life.

Was it always words for you?
It was always words for me.
My father made his living with words;
there was always popular music playing,
so the lyrics of songs were in my head.

Was it always words for you?
It was always words for me.
Looking back, the household's
preoccupation with language
nurtured my own.

Was it always words for you?
It was always words for me.
I listened to a thousand sermons
and memorized Bible verses.
Language mattered, indeed
language is a matter of life and death.

Was it always words for you?
It was always words for me.
Omnivorous attention,
relentless intelligence,
intense attention to words:
words have become quite active.

Was it always words for you?
It was always words for me.
A poem is not self-expression
but an act of listening,
a conversation packed with quotation,
quotable lines, self-reflection.

Was it always words for you?
It was always words for me.

www.ingramcontent.com/pod-product-compliance
Lightning Source LLC
Chambersburg PA
CBHW031158160426
43193CB00008B/419